THE LIFE OF
ZORA NEALE HURSTON

Author and Folklorist

Series Consultant:
Dr. Russell L. Adams, Chairman
Department of Afro-American Studies, Howard University

Della A. Yannuzzi

Enslow Publishers, Inc.
40 Industrial Road
Box 398
Berkeley Heights, NJ 07922
USA
        http://www.enslow.com

Dedicated to my daughter, Cara Ann

Originally published as *Zora Neale Hurston: Southern Storyteller* in 1996.

Library of Congress Cataloging-in-Publication Data

Yannuzzi, Della A.
    The life of Zora Neale Hurston : author and folklorist / Della A. Yannuzzi.
       pages cm. — (Legendary African Americans)
    Includes bibliographical references and index.
    ISBN 978-0-7660-6275-7
    1. Hurston, Zora Neale—Juvenile literature. 2. Authors, American--20th century—
Biography—Juvenile literature. 3. Folklorists—United States—Biography—Juvenile literature.
    4. Women and literature—Southern States—Juvenile literature. 5. Women and literature—
Southern States—Juvenile literature. 6. Southern States—In literature—Juvenile literature.
    I. Title.
    PS3515.U789Z9537 2015
    813'.52—dc23
    [B]

                                   2014027443

Future editions:
Paperback ISBN: 978-0-7660-6276-4
EPUB ISBN: 978-0-7660-6277-1
Single-User PDF ISBN: 978-0-7660-6278-8
Multi-User PDF ISBN: 978-0-7660-6279-5

Printed in the United States of America
102014 Bang Printing, Brainerd, Minn.
10 9 8 7 6 5 4 3 2 1

To Our Readers:
We have done our best to make sure all Internet Addresses in this book were active and appropriate
when we went to press. However, the author and the publisher have no control over and assume
no liability for the material available on those Internet sites or on other Web sites they may link to.
Any comments or suggestions can be sent by e-mail to comments@enslow.com or to the address on the
back cover.

♻ Enslow Publishers, Inc., is committed to printing our books on recycled paper. The paper in every
book contains 10% to 30% post-consumer waste (PCW). The cover board on the outside of each book
contains 100% PCW. Our goal is to do our part to help young people and the environment too!

Illustration Credits: Library of Congress, p. 4.

Cover Illustration: Library of Congress

CONTENTS

At the time of her death, many had forgotten about Zora Neale Hurston. But once her work was rediscovered, she became a woman who is considered one of the most influential American authors.

Chapter 1

NEW YORK, HERE I COME

When Zora Neale Hurston reached New York City in the winter of 1925, she had very little money and few clothes, no friends, and no prospect of a job. What this young southern African-American woman lacked in material wealth was balanced by a big talent and a strong will to succeed.

Hurston was a vivacious, tall woman who liked to wear colorful jewelry and eye-catching hats. In addition, she had a winning smile and a gift for storytelling. The combination of these traits held the attention of her listeners.

Hurston could not have arrived in New York at a better time, thanks to the emergence of the Harlem Renaissance, a movement that supported and encouraged African-American writers and artists. In her mind, there was no doubt that she could fulfill her potential as a fledgling writer in this northern city, even though she had been born and raised in Eatonville, a small all-black town in central Florida.

Surviving against all odds was nothing new to Hurston. She had been on her own since the age of fourteen, when she left home to work for a musical traveling troupe. The troupe performed amusing operettas created by the team of William Gilbert and Arthur Sullivan. In the twenty years she had been on her own, Hurston had managed to finish high school and earn an associate's degree from Howard University in Washington, D.C. She also made her writing debut in *Stylus*, Howard University's campus literary magazine.

While attending Howard University, Hurston had been encouraged by Dr. Alain Leroy Locke, the founder of the *Stylus* Literary Club, to submit some of her work to a magazine called *Opportunity: A Journal of Negro Life*, a publication of the National Urban League. The editor, Charles S. Johnson, had accepted one of her stories, "Drenched in Light," and had published it in the December 1924 issue. She had also submitted another story, "Spunk," and a play, *Color Struck*.

When Hurston was invited to attend the National Urban League's annual magazine awards dinner in New York City for her two nominated pieces, *Color Struck* and "Spunk," there were high expectations for her. Alain Locke had called her "the best and the brightest" of upcoming new writers.[1] Hurston herself had high hopes of winning a prize for her work, always remembering her mother's advice, to "jump at the sun."[2]

On the night of May 1, 1925, in a Fifth Avenue restaurant, Hurston was given two second prizes for her story "Spunk" and for her play *Color Struck*. Another young writer, Langston Hughes, won first prize for his poem "The Weary Blues."

After winning the coveted *Opportunity* award, Hurston stayed in New York and continued to write. In the fall of 1925, she won a scholarship to Barnard College, where she was the school's only African-American student. As was typical of her style, she was able to carve a place for herself in the all-white student body, and was well liked. In addition to studying English, Hurston also studied anthropology with a noted anthropologist, Franz Boas. Her study of different cultures had a significant impact on her writing. She was drawn to a serious study of African-American culture and folklore, which eventually became a dominant theme in her writing.

During her time in New York, Hurston met many aspiring and established writers. One of her closest friendships was with Langston Hughes. This young African-American poet and writer was born in Joplin, Missouri. Although Hughes's and Hurston's life experiences were very different, and Hurston was ten years older than Hughes, they were drawn to each other by their appreciation of each other's talent and ambition to succeed as writers. At the age of nineteen, Langston Hughes had already published his first poem, "The Negro Speaks of Rivers." Hurston was gaining recognition as a writer destined for big things.

Hurston carved a perfect niche for herself in the Harlem Renaissance era; she even was called Queen of the Renaissance, because she personified the excitement, talent, and enthusiasm of this important time in American history. She found a secretarial job with Fannie Hurst, a popular novelist of the time, and rented an apartment in Harlem. She often entertained other writers and artists with her retelling of southern folktales, including "lying stories" (tall tales), that she had heard from the adults in her hometown of Eatonville. Anyone who met Hurston could not deny that she was an unique individual who followed her own dreams.

Hurston had indeed become a "New Negro," a term used to describe members of the influential New York Harlem literary movement, which was an outlet for African Americans to express themselves through the arts. In a sense, the movement gave African Americans a forum for their talents and achievements. However, Hurston's wry sense of humor did not always amuse her colleagues. Her term for the New York African-American literary establishment was "Niggerati."

While Hurston had the ability to shock others and to bring humor into a situation, there were those who did not appreciate her outspokenness. She should not have been surprised, then, when her fiction was criticized for promoting a less than favorable picture of African Americans. Although Hurston did not understand or like the criticism directed at her work, she nevertheless continued to write in her own style, telling the stories of her people in the way she saw them.

In 1925, a book called *The New Negro* had been edited by Alain Locke. One of Hurston's stories, "Spunk," had been reprinted in this anthology of essays, poetry, and fiction. It received good reviews and perpetuated the view by African-American intellectuals such as Locke and Johnson that intelligent "artful" literature would liberate African Americans and lift them to higher elevations.

In response to *The New Negro*, Hurston and her fellow writers, including Langston Hughes, put together their own magazine, called *Fire!!*, which made its debut in November 1926 and ended with that same issue. One of Hurston's best stories, "Sweat," was published in *Fire!!* Although artistically superior to *The New Negro*, *Fire!!* shocked the literary establishment with its themes of sex and violence. Unfortunately, financial problems and disorganization within the group caused the quick demise of *Fire!!* In its short time, it brought further attention to this group of talented writers.

In the early 1920s, Zora Neale Hurston was definitely on her way to becoming a force in American literature. In addition, she also became a distinguished social scientist intent on preserving African-American folklore and culture.

In her autobiography, *Dust Tracks on a Road*, she wrote, "What waits for me in the future? I do not know. I cannot even imagine, and I am glad for that."[3]

Chapter 2

HOME—
EATONVILLE,
FLORIDA

Zora Neale Hurston was probably born on January 7, 1891 (no birth records survive), in Eatonville, Florida, to Lucy Ann Potts Hurston, a teacher, and John Hurston, a carpenter and a Baptist minister. Zora was the fifth child and second girl in a family of eight children. Her older sister, Sarah, was her father's favorite. He was content with his first daughter and three sons. As a matter of fact, he was not even around for Zora's birth, but off on one of his trips as a traveling preacher. The midwife was also out of town, so Zora was helped into the world by a white man who happened to be delivering a ham.

Zora's parents were very different from one another, but their love overcame their differences. At the age of twenty, John Hurston had noticed the diminutive fourteen-year-old Lucy at a church social. Lucy had also been attracted to the tall, handsome young man who kept staring at her from across the room.

Lucy Ann Potts' parents viewed Hurston as an Alabama sharecropper from the wrong side of the tracks, and not suitable marriage material for their well-to-do family. Lucy ignored her parents' warnings about getting involved with this older man. Although she was only fourteen years of age, she knew what she wanted, and that was John Hurston. Lucy Potts married John Hurston without her parents' blessings.

Together, Lucy and John Hurston made a remarkably good marriage. Hurston proved to be a hard worker with ambitions for getting ahead in life. Lucy Hurston was a strong woman who encouraged her husband in his endeavors.

Several years later, tired of working in the cotton fields of Alabama, Hurston moved his family, now including three children, to Eatonville, Florida. A small town ten miles north of Orlando, in Orange County, Eatonville was the first all-black self-governed town, incorporated in 1887. The town had lots of space for children to explore, lakes to swim in, and woods to run through. John

Hurston bought five acres of land abounding with tropical fruit trees, and he built a two-story, eight-room house. He and Lucy became solid citizens of Eatonville. She was a devoted wife and good mother who taught her children to read and write at an early age, and he was a compelling preacher and three-time mayor of Eatonville.

Zora flourished under the watchful eye of her mother and the close-knit protected environment of Eatonville. Her mother encouraged Zora's free spirit and independent nature. John Hurston, however, thought his daughter's outspokenness would get her into trouble with whites. Young Zora knew nothing of the racial strife abounding elsewhere in the state as well as in the rest of the country. She remained protected from racial discrimination.

From the time Zora was a young child, she had a curiosity and desire to see the world. She would sit on the gatepost in front of her house and ask passersby if she could travel down the road with them. Lucy Hurston admired her daughter's craving for knowledge, but John Hurston thought no good would come from her outspoken attitude.[1]

Zora was forever making up stories and plays. She enjoyed the company of her imagination even more than playing with children her own age.[2] She would tell her stories to her mother. Zora also claimed to be able to see into the future, and later in life, she felt she was able to form psychic bonds with people.

Zora attended the Hungerford School in Eatonville until she was thirteen years old. The Hungerford Normal and Industrial School was founded in 1889 by Robert F. Hungerford. In addition to normal studies, students were also instructed in human values, discipline, and hard work. Zora's teachers quickly noticed that she loved to read; she devoured the works of Hans Christian Andersen, Robert Louis Stevenson, and Rudyard Kipling.

Zora's vivid imagination was fueled by the stories she heard on the front porch of Joe Clarke's general store. In 1885, Clarke was the first African American to acquire land in Orange County, Florida. Leaders of Maitland, a town built by whites, helped Clarke start Eatonville. Eventually other parcels of land were sold to African Americans, and in 1887, the landowners filed for the town's incorporation. It seemed inevitable then that the adults of the town would gather on the porch of Joe Clarke, the town's first mayor, to tell their "lying stories" or folktales. These tales were passed down orally from generation to generation, but no one in the African-American community thought to record them on paper. After Zora left Eatonville, she never forgot those "lying tales," and later she traveled around the state and country in order to collect and record these precious stories.

When Zora was thirteen years old, a terrible event happened that would change her life forever. Her mother became ill with a terrible cold that probably developed into pneumonia. Zora waited for her mother to get out of bed, but it just did not happen. Zora spent many hours by her mother's bedside. Lucy confided in her daughter, telling her about some of the rituals practiced in their African-American culture. Lucy did not want certain of these practices carried out when she died; she did not feel they were necessary.[3] One was that a pillow placed beneath a dying person would prolong death, and therefore, it should be removed before the death occurred. Another one was that the clock in the room be covered, so that the rising soul did not become stuck in time at the moment of death.

Zora vowed to follow her mother's wishes, but at the time of Lucy Potts Hurston's death, Zora was held back by her father. In keeping with tradition, her mother's pillow was removed, and the clock was covered. When Zora protested, John Hurston led his strong-willed daughter away. She never forgot this traumatic experience, and she learned from it that cultural beliefs could have a strong effect on people.

A few weeks later, Zora was sent to Jacksonville, Florida, to attend a boarding school. Her sister, Sarah, and brother Bob were already there. Leaving Eatonville was a rude awakening for Zora. She was now in a white people's world, where the rules were very different.

Although Zora excelled in school, she was lonely. Sarah decided to return home; she wrote a letter to Zora telling her that their father had remarried, but all was not well. The once joyful, well-run household was presided over by their new stepmother, who did not want any part of the Hurston children. She was particularly jealous of her husband's relationship with Sarah, and wanted her out of the house.[4] Consequently, Sarah rushed into marriage, taking her youngest brother to live with her and her new husband.

John Hurston at first did not stand up to his second wife. Without Lucy's strength and guidance, he floundered. He silently watched his beloved Sarah leave; their relationship was forever damaged. Zora was angry that this strange woman had been allowed into their home, upsetting the stable family life they had once shared.[5] She vowed to get even one day, and she had her chance a few years later, when she and her stepmother had it out in a hair-pulling fight.

Chapter 3

IT'S A HARD LIFE

Zora was surprised when the director of her Jacksonville school told her that her father was late in making her school payments.[1] The director explained that in order for her to continue her studies at the school, she would have to help pay for her own tuition. Since Zora did not have any money of her own, she was put to work in the school kitchen or anywhere else she was needed, so she could earn her way. As if this were not difficult enough, Zora was told at the end of the school year that her father had written to the school asking if it would like to adopt her. Even though Zora had never been close to her father, she just could not believe that he would put his own daughter up for adoption.

The school could not adopt Zora; children cannot be adopted by institutions. Instead, the director paid for the trip back to Eatonville. Soon after Zora arrived, she realized that the two-story house with its chinaberry bushes and fruit trees was not the same home she had remembered. It had become a dark and lonely place, devoid of laughter and lively conversation. Zora's stepmother did not want John Hurston's children or the responsibility of raising a family. John Hurston and his wife divorced a few years later, but it was too late for his children. They had been separated from each other and were out on their own or living in the homes of friends.

It was not a happy time for the fourteen-year-old girl. At this young age, Zora felt that she was on her own. Going back to school was out of the question because she had no tuition money, so Zora began looking for ways to support herself. The only jobs she was able to get with her limited education were maid or waitress jobs. Zora never held these jobs for very long, because her thoughts were always on other things. She was a bright and thoughtful girl, interested in reading books and educating herself. She was always daydreaming about traveling to faraway places and doing exciting things.

One job Zora enjoyed was as an upstairs maid for a wealthy white couple. The woman of the house, Miss Alice, liked Zora, and so did the couple's two young daughters. The only trouble was that Zora preferred entertaining the children to cleaning the bedrooms. She would spend hours telling them stories and playing with them. The children's mother liked having Zora around, because this gave her more freedom, but the head cook of the house, a big woman called Miz Cally, complained that Zora was not doing her work. Zora called Miz Cally the "president of the kitchen" because she carried a lot of weight in the household, both personally and physically. Miz Cally had been with the family for many years, and she did not like Zora coming in and stirring things up. She thought Zora was too young and inexperienced for her job, and she resented Zora for leaving her work undone so she could entertain the children. She complained to the children's father that the new girl was not working out. Since Miz Cally had been with him since he was born, he did not ignore her unhappiness. Against the children's wishes, Zora was fired.

Zora knew that cleaning houses was not for her. She was sure that there had to be something more exciting in her future. When her brother Bob asked Zora to live with him and his family in 1906, she jumped at the chance. At last, she would have a home again. Bob even said she might be able to go back to school. With high expectations, Zora packed her few belongings and left Eatonville. Unfortunately, Zora's sister-in-law had different plans for her. She objected to Zora's just staying with them and not earning her keep. Before long, Zora found herself baby-sitting for her brother's children. She did not mind doing this, but her plans to go back to school never materialized. She found herself taking care of the house and the children, the same things she had been doing in Eatonville.

One day, Zora had a little bit of luck. She had made friends with a white woman whose husband told her about a job opening with a Gilbert and Sullivan acting troupe. Ironically, it was another maid's job, but this time it was as a personal lady's maid to "Miss M," a kind and gentle actress. Zora thanked her friend and went for an interview. Although Miss M thought Zora was too young, she still hired her because of Zora's outgoing and pleasant manner. When Zora found out the pay was $10 a week plus expenses, she quickly accepted the job.

During the early 1900s, $10 a week was a lot of money. Everyone in the troupe liked Zora's bubbling personality and gift for telling Eatonville stories. She stayed with the touring company for nearly two years until Miss M left to get married.

The troupe was in Baltimore when Miss M announced her engagement. Miss M wished Zora luck and happiness and promised to write her letters. Once again, Zora found herself on her own, without the comfort and security of a supporting cast of friends.

Zora carefully considered her options, and she decided to find another job and go back to school. Unfortunately, she had a setback when she came down with appendicitis and had to have surgery. It was a frightening experience, but Zora was young and strong; she healed quickly. When she was well again, she found a waitress job and in 1917, she enrolled in the high school division of Baltimore's Morgan Academy.

William Pickens, the dean of Morgan Academy, was so impressed with Zora Neale Hurston's entrance examination that she was given credit for two years of high school. He also found her a live-in job with Dr. Baldwin, one of the trustees of Morgan. Hurston was paid $2 a week (enough to attend school) to look after Dr. Baldwin's invalid wife. Her pay included a room and meals, as well as the use of the Baldwins' well-stocked library. Years later, she wrote in her autobiography, "I had hundreds of books under my skin already, but I read so much lest I never get a chance to read again!"[2]

Hurston worked hard at her studies, and earned high grades in her English classes. Although she could not afford to dress as well as the other students did, she made up for her lack of funds with her ready smile and clever mind. She never felt "shoved around" by the well-to-do students from Baltimore's best families.[3]

Hurston spent two years at Morgan, and would have liked to continue her education at the school. However, through her acquaintance with the Hughes family, who were Morgan trustees, she met the daughter of sociologist Dr. Kelly Miller, of Howard University. Mae Miller suggested that Hurston apply to the prestigious African-American college in Washington, D.C. She was accepted and was able to support herself and pay for her studies by working as a waitress and a manicurist.

Hurston's life as a promising writer began at Howard University. She excelled in her studies under teachers who recognized her unique talent for storytelling. She was accepted into The Stylus, a small literary group that was headed by Dr. Alain Leroy Locke, who had been the first African-American Rhodes Scholar at Oxford University. Dr. Locke was an important influence in Hurston's development as a writer. Under Dr. Locke's guidance, Hurston's "John Redding Goes to Sea" was printed in the May 1921 issue of *Stylus* magazine. Charles S. Johnson, the founder of *Opportunity* magazine in

New York, read it and instantly recognized Hurston's unique talent as a storyteller. He later published her stories "Drenched in Light" and "Spunk," which led to her first big break into the literary scene.

It seemed, at last, that Zora Neale Hurston's life was now taking a turn for the better. College had given her direction and friends, and her literary skills were leading her to a promising writing career. Her personal life was also improving. While she was at Howard, she met a premed student named Herbert Sheen. They fell in love and started to plan a future together. Although Sheen left Howard in 1921 to enter the University of Chicago, he and Hurston tried to remain close. They wrote often to each other, waiting for the day when they could be together again.

Chapter 4

A LITERARY AND ACADEMIC WORLD

By 1925, at age thirty-four, Hurston was contentedly settled into a literary and academic life. She had finished her education at Howard University and had moved to New York. The Harlem literary community accepted her with open arms, yet she was not without her critics. Although she was praised for her writing abilities, Hurston's work was criticized for its usage of African-American idioms and primitive folklore. Hurston's view of her people, however, was that they were a natural and beautiful people whose language and culture were as rich and unique as those of any other culture. It was with this sense of appreciation that Hurston chose to portray the "down-home" folk in her fiction, showing that they experienced the same feelings and thoughts shared by all humankind.

Of course, this view of her race did not sit well with many of her peers, who saw Hurston's fiction as an obstacle to the uplifting of African Americans to a higher level of achievement. She was accused of being apathetic about the problems African Americans experienced. Her critics claimed that she was not addressing the real issues of poverty, prejudice, and a lack of education that were keeping her people down. Hurston denied these claims, upset that these critics did not understand that she was celebrating the African-American community, and not tearing it down.

Despite this criticism, Hurston thrived in the midst of the Harlem Renaissance. Her personal style, intelligence, and flair for fun fit in perfectly with the glitter and richness of this important movement. She was just as glad to attend a festive party, or dance the night away at a popular night spot, as she was to settle down to some serious work at a literary club meeting. Hurston enjoyed both being entertained and being the entertainer. Langston Hughes remembered that Hurston was always full of stories and tales and had the ability to be quite amusing.[1]

During this time, Hurston formed some lasting friendships. In her autobiography, *Dust Tracks on a Road*, she says, "[Friendship] is a wonderful trade, a noble thing for anyone to work at."[2]

One of her most enduring friendships was with the novelist Fannie Hurst, who had been a contest judge at the *Opportunity* awards dinner. Hurst offered her a job as a live-in secretary. Hurston, always in need of money and a place to stay, gratefully agreed, although she was not very good at typing or shorthand. Hurst soon realized that Hurston would never become a proficient secretary, but she liked this talented, friendly writer and kept her on as a companion and occasional driver. On the other hand, Hurston tolerated the popular novelist's moods, which ranged from playfulness to sullenness. Hurston had the ability to look beneath a person's facade and discover the real human being. She judged people not by their race or color, but as one human interacting with another.

The match between them was a good one, and the writers formed a bond of friendship that lasted for years. They often traveled together, with Hurst making the plans and Hurston driving. One trip that Hurston wrote about in her autobiography was a two-week car tour through Ontario, Canada. Hurston said of her friend that "she was like a child at a circus. She was a run-away, with no responsibilities. . . . Then she replaced Mrs. Hurst's little Fannie and began to discuss her next book with me and got very serious in her manner."[3]

Hurston formed another lasting friendship with the singer and actress Ethel Waters. Hurston had written Waters several letters, which went unanswered until a dinner was given for Hurston to which Waters was invited. Hurston was pleased to learn that Waters had not meant to ignore her, but that she was a private person and did not see what they could possibly have in common. When they did meet, they hit it off and remained good friends.

In addition to the good things happening in Hurston's personal life, her academic life was also advancing. Hurston came to the attention of Annie Nathan Meyer, one of the founders of Barnard College, the women's division of Columbia University. Hurston had met Meyer at the *Opportunity* awards dinner, and soon after that, Meyer arranged for a Barnard scholar- ship for Hurston. In the fall of 1925, she began her Barnard studies, taking English courses, but also developing an interest in anthropology after she signed up for a course with noted anthropologist

Franz Boas. At the time, Hurston did not know that the study of anthropology would add new dimensions to her writing.

Papa Boas, as Hurston called him, opened new doors for her into the exciting world of African-American culture and folklore. Through the study of her culture, Hurston developed a deeper academic understanding of her race, and later, she celebrated the uniqueness of the African-American culture in her writing. The stories she had heard on Joe Clarke's porch, and the life she had lived in Eatonville, would forever be entwined in her work.

In February 1927, with most of her college work completed, Hurston was granted a fellowship by the Association for the Study of Negro Life and History for a field trip to the South. Papa Boas had helped arrange the finances for this trip, so his student could begin collecting African-American folklore. Hurston then took a train to Jacksonville, Florida, and bought a car, which she named Sassie Susie. While driving through the South, she stopped in Memphis, Tennessee, to visit her brother Bob, who was now a doctor. They reminisced about their father, John Hurston, who had been killed in an auto accident in 1917. They both agreed that his life had not gone smoothly after the death of their mother, and that John Hurston had regretted his treatment of his children. Later, Hurston penned in her autobiography that "We were all sorry for him, instead of feeling bitter as might have been expected. Old Maker had left out the steering gear when He gave Papa his talents."[4]

After visiting with Bob, she drove to see her brother Ben, who was now a pharmacist. They exchanged news about the rest of the family. Another brother, Clifford Joel, was the principal of an African-American high school. Another brother, John, was a grocery store owner. The youngest brother, Everett, was working in a post office in Brooklyn, New York.

After visiting her brothers, Hurston was in high spirits. She had not felt this close to her family since her mother's death. Always an independent, proud woman, Hurston did not want to burden her siblings with her own problems, but she remained in contact with them and their children.

Eager to get started on a folklore project, Hurston drove to New Orleans, Louisiana, where she dove into the job of collecting southern African-American folklore. It was not an easy task, however. Although Hurston was a witty and gregarious person, she had difficulty getting her folklore sources to confide in her. She was well aware of the importance of this trip, which had both social and historical significance. As an educated African-American woman, Hurston was in the unique position of being able to contribute to the serious study of African-American folklore and culture. She would find some way to communicate with the people.

Chapter 5

In New Directions

By the spring of 1927, Hurston decided she needed a break from the arduous task of gathering southern black folklore. She did not want to disappoint Papa Boas or the Association for the Study of Negro Life and History, which had sponsored her fellowship, but she decided that she was not using the right approach. Instead of relating to the people in a language they understood, she was presenting the image of an all-knowing academic. She needed time to refine her collecting methods. With this in mind, Hurston planned to go back to New York and get advice from Boas, but before she did, she drove to St. Augustine, Florida. On May 19, 1927, she married Herbert Sheen, her longtime friend.

The marriage seemed doomed from the start. In one biography of Hurston, the author recounts that she had doubts from the beginning, and had even dreamed that a "dark shadow" was looming over the marriage ceremony.[1] As a matter of fact, Hurston's work always was more important to her than any of her relationships. This inevitably caused problems.

While Sheen expected his bride to put him and his medical career ahead of her own interests, Hurston's attention was focused on her own work. By August 1927, only three months after her marriage, Hurston was on her way back to New York. She was accompanied by Langston Hughes, whom she had met by chance on a trip to Mobile, Alabama. Sheen had already gone back to medical school in Chicago.

The ride back to New York City proved to be a pleasant experience for both Hurston and Hughes. They enjoyed each other's company and talked about working together on a play.[2] In their conversations, Hughes mentioned a woman who was helping him financially. Charlotte van der Veer Quick Mason, a wealthy white widow, was a valued patron of the arts and was especially supportive of African-American artists and writers. Hurston listened carefully to Hughes, who admired Mason's keen interest in the arts—he called her Godmother, at her request. She decided to meet Charlotte Mason as soon as possible.

When Hughes and Hurston finally reached New York, she immediately went to see Franz Boas, who was concerned about the incomplete material she had been sending him. In the meantime, Hughes had paid a visit to Charlotte Mason and had told her about Hurston. His enthusiastic description of his friend aroused Mason's curiosity, which in turn prompted Mason to invite Hurston to visit her Park Avenue home.

Hurston, of course, accepted the invitation. Since no additional financial aid was forthcoming from the Association for the Study of Negro Life and History, Hurston was eager to meet this rich patron. In mid- September 1927, Hurston accepted Mason's invitation. They got along well at this first meeting. Hurston told Mason about the play she and Hughes were planning to work on, and she talked about her interest in African-American folklore and culture. Mason expressed an interest in the "real folk," and the naturalness of the "Negro farthest down."[3] Hurston left the meeting confident that she and Godmother could work together.

By December, Hurston had signed a contract with Mason that enabled her to return to the South for another year of folklore collecting. Mason agreed to finance Hurston's trip in return for a written report and the approval of and publishing rights to all material gathered by Hurston.

Although Hurston respected Mason for her ideas and patronage, she also felt restrained by the wealthy widow's tight controls. For example, Mason did not want to support Hurston in her own commercial endeavors as a writer. She wanted Hurston to act as her employee, collecting material for her. Mason would then decide what to do with it. In other words, because Hurston was not a free agent, she could not sell any work in book form until Mason approved it. One of Mason's favorite sayings, which she used when she was displeased, was "It has no soul in it."[4] She set high standards, and demanded that her protégés follow them strictly.

Hurston was well aware of these conditions because they were written into her contract. The promise of $200 a month for a year, as well as an automobile and a camera, was too good a deal for her to turn down. Unfortunately, throughout her life, Hurston always needed an outside source of money in order to continue with her work. Her writing never produced a steady flow of income for her.

During Hurston and Mason's five-year relationship, Mason contributed about $15,000 to Hurston's research work, in return for exclusive rights to all collected material. Mason also stipulated in the contract that Hurston tell no one else about this material unless Mason gave permission.

Now that Hurston had Mason's financial support, she lost no time in getting on with her research. In December 1927, she was on her way to Florida. She spent some time in Eatonville, then headed to Polk County, where she hoped to discover real stories in infamous juke joints or bawdy lumber camp social clubs, where workers gathered to let off steam. She had high expectations of finding a gold mine of information in these places.

The Everglades Cypress Lumber Company, near Loughman, Florida, was known as one of the toughest camps around. The population of these camps ranged from honest working families to dishonest thugs and criminals. The inhabitants of these camps viewed strangers with suspicion. In order to be accepted into these camps, Hurston had to tell them that she was a "woman on the run."[5]

Gaining the confidence of these distrustful strangers was a tall order for Hurston, but she was creative in seeking out ways to get those "lying stories." Once she announced a contest, with prizes for the four best lies. The response was overwhelming.

Another valuable source for Hurston came in the form of a woman called Big Sweet, whose large size earned her considerable respect. She took a liking to Hurston and led her to some valuable sources. In addition, Big Sweet became Hurston's protector. The juke joints were rough places, where emotions ran high, but as long as Big Sweet was around, Hurston was safe.

Hurston would have continued her research work at the lumber camp if her visit had not been cut short by a jealous woman named Lucy. One day Lucy announced she was going to "hurt" Hurston for paying too much attention to Slim, Lucy's one-time boyfriend. Actually, Slim had only been a good source of information for Hurston, but Lucy did not want to believe that. She lunged at Hurston with a knife, surprising even Big Sweet. Hurston remembered Big Sweet "sprang like a lioness" to her defense, giving Hurston just enough time to get out the door.[6] Hurston hurriedly packed her suitcase and drove Sassie Susie to her next destination, the city of New Orleans, Louisiana.

When Hurston arrived in New Orleans in August 1928, she was ready to learn about the magical and mysterious world of hoodoo, a variation of voodoo, a form of worship with African religious origins. It is believed that through the power of a hoodoo doctor and magical forces, certain illnesses can be treated, and special spells can be cast that are thought to bring about good or bad luck.

Hurston literally threw herself body and soul into learning about and experiencing the effects of hoodoo religion. She studied with different hoodoo doctors and participated in various ceremonies. One notable doctor, Luke Turner, endowed her with a crown of power (coil of snakeskins) that she would have to earn in a special ceremony. For three days, Hurston lay unclothed on a couch, with nothing but a rattlesnake skin covering her. She was not allowed to eat or drink and was told to remain silent so that her soul would be accepted by the spirit of the altar. According to her autobiography, "on the second day I began to dream strange exalted dreams. . . . In one I strode across the heavens with lightning flashing from under my feet."[7] Her participation in these ceremonies showed the extent of Hurston's ability to research her material thoroughly. She did not describe the specific secret details of these experiences, but it is plain that they influenced her greatly.

Hurston stayed in Louisiana until the spring of 1929. At that time, she traveled back to Florida, where she visited her brother John. She then rented a cabin in Eau Gallie, a town near Saint Augustine, Florida, where she sorted through her varied collection of folklore material and began the rewriting process. Her plan had been to travel to Miami for another collecting session, but she became ill with a stomach ailment and had to enter the hospital. She recovered enough by August 1929 to leave for Miami.

Hurston had proven long ago that she had a wandering spirit. When she was a small girl, she would swing on her house gate and ask passing travelers if she could ride up the road with them. Now, at the age of thirty-eight, she was still moving from one place to another, always searching for more excitement and adventure.

After staying in Miami for about two months, she decided to move on to the island of Nassau, in the Bahamas. Her curiosity had been aroused by the Bahamian music she had heard while she was in Florida. The trip to Nassau was a success; she collected more than a hundred tunes. Hurston was so impressed with the Bahamian songs and dances that she vowed to introduce them to the rest of the world. For several years, Hurston organized and produced concerts of African-American dance and song. She would have continued if she had more financial support, but, at the time, she felt compelled to write.

Chapter 6

THE *MULE BONE* CONTROVERSY

n the winter of 1930, Zora Neale Hurston and Langston Hughes were comfortably situated in a rooming house in Westfield, New Jersey. This was made possible by their benefactor, Charlotte Mason. Mason was very much in control of the literary careers of both her protégés, and she wanted the writers to have a quiet place to work on their present projects.

Hurston was expected to spend time on her folklore collections, as well as on organizing the Bahamian songs. Hughes was putting the finishing touches on his first novel, *Not Without Laughter*, which would later win him the Harmon Gold Award for literature. At this time, Hurston and Hughes also began serious work on a play based on a tale Hurston had collected in Eatonville. She had written a short story, "The Bone of Contention," based on this tale. *Mule Bone* began as an African-American folk opera, but soon changed into a folk comedy. The intent of the play was to portray African-American characters as a strong race of people capable of weathering their misfortunes through the use of humor.

In addition to paying for their expenses, Mason had also hired a former teacher, Louise Thompson, to work for them as a secretary and typist. In the beginning, the trio appeared to work well together, yet within a short time, disharmony arose in the group, mainly between Hughes and Hurston. Their disagreement centered around Louise Thompson.

In May 1930, Hurston decided to leave Westfield. She was headed south again, hoping to finish her portion of work on *Mule Bone*. At the time, she did not speak about her growing dissatisfaction, but secretly she was resentful, mainly toward Hughes, but toward Thompson as well. It appeared to Hurston that Hughes was considering Thompson as an equal partner in the writing of *Mule Bone*, while Hurston saw Thompson's function strictly as that of a typist. To make matters worse, Mason approved of Thompson's involvement, which only complicated matters further.

Langston Hughes was having his own difficulties with Godmother. Mason was exercising more and more control over Hughes' work. In addition, Mason was angry with him over a poem Hughes had written called "Advertisement for the Waldorf-Astoria." Mason thought the poem criticized the lifestyles of the wealthy.[1] These differences caused a bitter parting between them, after which Hughes returned to his mother's home in Cleveland, Ohio.

Soon after reaching Cleveland, Hughes found out that *Mule Bone* was going to be staged without his consent. He telephoned Hurston, who told him she knew nothing about this rumor. Hughes did not believe her. Later, Hurston found out that a friend, Carl Van Vechten, had a copy of the comedy and had sent it to a producer. Hughes insisted that his name also be on the play, since he had coauthored it with her. Hurston retaliated, saying that the idea had been hers from the beginning.[2]

In order to protect his interests, Hughes sent a copy of the play to the United States copyright office, listing his and Hurston's names as the authors. Again in rebuttal, Hurston then wrote a letter to Hughes. She thought it unfair that Hughes wanted to split proceeds from the play with Thompson, who had been hired by Mason to be their typist. She also thought it wrong that Hughes wanted Thompson to become the business manager of the play's production. To strengthen her own position,

Hurston also stated that Mason approved of the latest version of the play, and that she agreed that it had been rewritten by Hurston and no one else.[3]

Langston Hughes threatened to sue Zora Neale Hurston. Many letters were exchanged between the writers and their lawyers in an effort to resolve their differences. At one point, in early February 1932, it appeared that the play would be performed in Cleveland, Ohio. However, Hurston found out that Louise Thompson had visited Hughes. Hurston immediately went to Hughes' home and confronted him about Thompson's visit. Langston Hughes was ill with the flu and did not respond to Hurston's charges. Nothing was resolved, except that Hurston canceled the theater production of *Mule Bone*.

There were two significant results of the *Mule Bone* disagreement. One was the breakup of a promising professional and social friendship between Langston Hughes and Zora Neale Hurston. The second was the loss of an opportunity to create an important stage production for the African-American theater. Hurston's early dreams of establishing an African-American theater with Langston Hughes ended on that cold February night. As Henry Louis Gates, Jr., said in his introduction to the 1991 edition of *Mule Bone: A Comedy of Negro Life*:

With Hurston's mastery of the vernacular and compelling sense of story, and Hughes's impressive sense of poetic and theatrical structure, it would have been difficult to imagine a more ideal team to construct "a real Negro theater."[4]

Mule Bone remained unperformed for many years due to the lack of communication and trust between Hurston and Hughes. Fortunately, the typescript of *Mule Bone* has survived. It is not known exactly who wrote which part, but scholars have agreed that acts one and three, and perhaps one scene of the second act, were a collaboration by both writers. Finally, in February 1991, some sixty years after it was written, *Mule Bone: A Comedy of Negro* Life was performed at Lincoln Center in New York City.

The year 1931 proved to be one of dramatic change for Hurston. In addition to the *Mule Bone* fiasco, in March of that same year, less than a year after Hughes and Mason had parted company, Hurston and Charlotte Mason ended their complicated five-year relationship. Hurston's contract had ended, and neither wanted to renew it. Although Hurston was indebted to Mason for her financial support, she was no longer willing to put up with Mason's interference or with her right to control Hurston's work. Finally free of Mason's literary control, Hurston struck out on her own.

In July, Zora Hurston severed ties with another important person in her life. She and Herbert Sheen were divorced after four years of marriage.

Although the *Mule Bone* incident did not end well, Hurston came out of the experience convinced that the stories of African-American life should be interpreted on the stage through colorful language, movement, dance, and song. Although Hurston had collected an amazing array of folk material ranging from songs, games, and stories to interpretive dance, she was unable to interest anyone in publishing this material in its current form. She then decided the material should be performed onstage, and began looking for someone to produce it for the theater.

Hurston began contacting people who had expressed interest in her theatrical ideas. Her first effort, for which she wrote three sketches, was *Fast and Furious*, a revue—a series of short plays, songs, and dances. She also had a part in it, playing a pom-pom girl at a football game. Unfortunately, *Fast and Furious* received poor reviews and closed in a week. In order to gain experience in the theater, Hurston wrote sketches for other revues. She wanted more creative control over her own work, so she decided to produce her own show, using the wealth of folklore she had collected. The play was written as a re-creation of a day in the life of railroad camp workers, using their own words and movements.

Since money was always a problem for Hurston, she had to sell her car and ask Mason for a loan in order to rent a theater and to pay for costumes, singers, and dancers.

The revue was called *The Great Day*, and it was staged on January 10, 1932, at the John Golden Theater in New York City. Although *The Great Day* did not earn much money for Hurston, it did receive excellent reviews for its naturalness of movement and song. Hurston had hoped to get more financial backing so the play could continue, but without any additional funds forthcoming, Hurston's *The Great Day* had only one performance at that theater.

In addition to the lack of money, Hurston had another problem. Charlotte Mason still held the legal rights to Hurston's material, and she did not approve of its commercial use. Nevertheless, Hurston continued to fight for more literary freedom. Mason finally agreed to give Hurston some rights to the material from which *The Great Day* was taken. Hurston gratefully accepted, and whenever she could raise the money, she staged additional performances. She kept *The Great Day* going for three years.

Finally, Mason told Hurston that she could not finance any more drama projects because of her own financial problems. She gave Hurston enough money to buy a pair of shoes and the fare to

Eatonville so she could continue work on *Mules and Men*. Hurston then headed back to Florida, but she was not ready to give up on her revues. She had high hopes of creating an African-American theater in the South, even though all odds were against her. Somehow, she managed to interest Robert Wunsch of the English Department at Rollins College in Winter Park, Florida, to stage another performance of *The Great Day*. This time, the revue was called *From Sun to Sun*. The performance was a success, and a second show was scheduled.

For several years, Zora Neale Hurston organized and produced revues of African-American dance and song, while still pursuing her writing career. However, it seemed that theatrical production was not to be Hurston's main interest. Finding financial backing for her productions had become too difficult, and she could not always raise the money herself. She decided to concentrate fully on her literary efforts, and she began with the "lying stories" she had heard on Joe Clarke's porch.

Chapter 7

THE WRITING LIFE

The early 1930s was an intense period of writing for Hurston. She was still very much interested in organizing revues, but without continued financial backing, she could not put all of her energy into this one area. Back in New York, Hurston focused on her writing, appealing to Charlotte Mason for funds in order to keep going. Although Mason had not renewed Hurston's contract, she had invested many years of interest in the writer. She continued to give her money upon request, but she made it clear that she could not keep financing Hurston's work indefinitely.

Thankful for whatever help she received, Hurston continued to work on her manuscript of African-American folklore, while looking for a publisher for the book she called *Mules and Men*. Although Mason still had control over much of the material, Hurston hoped that one day Mason would relinquish all her rights as stated in their former contract. Then Hurston would be able to find someone interested in publishing her "lying stories" with titles such as "Why We Have Gophers," "How the Cat Got 9 Lives," and "How the Possum Lost the Hair Off His Tail."

In the spring of 1932, Hurston once again left for Florida and her hometown of Eatonville. In July 1932, *Mules and Men* was completed. She still needed to persuade Charlotte Mason to give her control over her material, and then she could find a publisher. In the meantime, Hurston returned to fiction writing. She wrote a short story called "The Gilded Six-Bits" (six bits equal seventy-five cents), which was published in *Story* magazine. "The Gilded Six-Bits," set in Eatonville, tells the story of a young wife named Missie May, who is attracted to another man partly because of the gold piece on his watch charm. The irony of the story is that the gold piece turns out to be a gilded half-dollar. Missy feels foolish, but her husband, Joe, forgives his gullible wife, and buys her some candy kisses with the gilded six-bits as proof of his forgiveness.

This story is considered one of Hurston's finest, and it was responsible for attracting the attention of Bertram Lippincott, a noted book publisher. Lippincott wrote a letter to Hurston inquiring whether she had a book manuscript for him to see. Hurston wrote back, saying that she was working on a book. In fact, she had only the idea and not a word on paper.[1]

This detail was not about to deter Hurston. She immediately moved to Sanford, Florida, so she could concentrate more fully on her work. She was virtually penniless, but she managed to rent a one-room house for $1.50 a week, living on $.50 a week, which she borrowed from a cousin. By early September 1933, Hurston had finished her first novel, *Jonah's Gourd Vine*. It had taken her a little more than two months to write it. She then had it typed and mailed it out to Lippincott. This was easier said than done, because Hurston had run out of money. Falling back on her own ingenuity, and with a little luck, she managed to hire a woman to type the manuscript, promising to pay later. She then borrowed $2 from the treasurer of the local Daughters of Elks to use for postage.

At this time, Hurston owed $18 in back rent on the house where she lived in Sanford. She hoped to pay this with some money she was owed from the booking of some vocalists for a city concert.[2] Unfortunately, the landlady was not willing to wait for her money, and Hurston found herself out on the street, wearing a pair of old worn-out shoes and carrying the few clothes she owned. When the money from the concert booking came through, Hurston hurried to the shoe store and bought herself a new pair of shoes. While she was there, she opened a Western Union wire she had received earlier in the day but had not had time to read. The wire was from J. B. Lippincott. They had accepted her book and offered her an advance of $200. She could not run fast enough to the Western Union office to accept Lippincott's offer.

In May of 1934, Hurston's first novel, *Jonah's Gourd Vine*, was published. Critics agree that this novel is autobiographical. It is set in Eatonville, Florida, and its main characters are John Pearson, a preacher with a wandering eye, and his strong-willed wife, Lucy, who tries to keep her husband headed in the right direction. It was no coincidence that Hurston's father, John, was a preacher, and that Lucy, his wife, was the guiding force in Hurston's own family.

The book received mixed reviews. One review, published in *Opportunity* magazine in August 1934, stated:

Miss Hurston approached her task with a knowledge of Negro dialect and customs that is rare in contemporary writers. . . . Although Miss Hurston has the ability to paint clear and vivid pictures of Negro life, her style at times falls flat.[3]

Another review, published in *The New York Times* in May 1934, said, "Not the least charm of the book, however, is its language: rich, expressive, and lacking in self-conscious artifice."[4]

Hurston welcomed the attention, even if some of it was negative. Yet, she was well aware that the $200 advance would not last forever. Once again, later in 1934, she had to find a source of income. She decided to try booking her revue, *From Sun to Sun*, around the Florida area, and was fairly successful at this attempt. Her work soon came to the attention of Mary McLeod Bethune, president of Bethune-Cookman College in Daytona Beach, Florida.

Bethune was the founder of the National Council of Negro Women, and had developed the college from a girl's training school. When Bethune approached Hurston to help form a school of "dramatic Negro expression," the idea certainly appealed to her.[5] However, on a personal level, she and Bethune did not get along. This was due in part to their similar personalities. Both Hurston and Bethune were independent, strong-willed people, with definite ideas of how things should progress.

Bethune, of course, had more power and authority as president of the college. Hurston, on the other hand, felt she had more experience with the creative arts but was not being given the cooperation or authority she needed in order to do a good job. Although she did put on a successful show of *From Sun to Sun* using Bethune-Cookman's student body, the development of a creative school of black expression never materialized. Hurston left the college, and, once again, she turned her attention to preparing *Mules and Men* for publication. Mason had agreed to release her control over the folklore material, which gave Hurston freedom to offer it to Lippincott. The book was published in 1935.

During this time, Hurston was, in fact, working at two jobs. Most of the time she wrote, but when she was in need of money, Hurston tried to stage a revue. She strongly believed that song and movement would show the innate beauty and naturalness of the African American in the theatrical arts. However, many middle- and upper-class African Americans did not view Hurston's dance and song productions as helpful to an advancement of the race. Some of those who reviewed her concerts saw them as "primitive," while Hurston saw these productions of African-American drama as powerful and unique, something that was distinctly their own.[6]

Hurston found a lack of support for her concerts not only in the general population, but also within the academic community. This criticism prompted Hurston to reevaluate her presentation of African-American folklore. Would these expressions of her culture be taken more seriously if she had an advanced degree?

With this thought in mind, in late 1934, she decided to apply for a scholarship to Columbia University, where she wanted to work toward a doctorate degree in anthropology and folklore. Hurston had good intentions, but she never earned an advanced degree, for several reasons: One reason was her old adversary, money. Another reason was her reason for wanting a doctorate degree. Hurston had wanted credibility to be attached to her study of African-American folklore. More specifically, she wanted this folklore to be expressed through the art forms of drama and music. She was not interested in seeing this material presented in too scientific a manner, issued only as unreadable books. She wanted her material to have a practical application, for all people to enjoy and appreciate it.

Nevertheless, Hurston was eager to begin a program of study. She asked Franz Boas, her old anthropology professor, to help her, and together they worked out a plan that included a field trip to Haiti.

Financial help had been promised to her by the Julius Rosenwald Foundation, an organization known to be generous in its support of African-American students. However, Hurston's relationship with the Rosenwald Foundation was shaky. Hurston and the foundation could never mutually agree on a program of study, or on the distribution of funds. Eventually, monies were withdrawn not long after she began her studies. In the end, Hurston decided that her efforts would be best directed toward her writing and gave up the idea of studying at Columbia. From this point on, her work on African-American culture became less formal.

During this period, two events were taking up much of Hurston's energy: One was the scheduled publication of her book *Mules and Men* and the other was her relationship with a young man she identified in her autobiography only by the initials A. W. P. She said, "I did not just fall in love. I made a parachute jump. No matter which way I probed him, I found something more to admire."[7]

All should have been well, but it was not. A. W. P. wanted Hurston to give up her career and marry him. Hurston would not do this. Another obstacle standing between them was their lack of trust in each other. They were never secure in each other's commitment to the other, always believing that someone else would lure each away from the other. They were unwilling to give each other up, until

Hurston finally realized that there could be no compromise. As in her marriage to Herbert Sheen, Hurston could not reconcile her work with a close relationship. When she was awarded a Guggenheim Fellowship to continue her fieldwork, Hurston gratefully accepted it. This gave her the opportunity to get away from A. W. P.

Chapter 8

DIFFERENT WORLDS

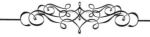

Hurston could not stay in one place for too long; the desire to travel never left her. It was as though she never grew up, remaining forever that child who longed to see those worlds outside of Eatonville.

Always eager to visit new places, and in an effort to forget A. W. P., Hurston embarked for Kingston, Jamaica, in April 1936. For about six months, she lived with the Maroons, a group of descendants of people who had rebelled against slavery. Their homes were in the remote mountain areas of Jamaica, near Accompong. Hurston lived among them, patiently waiting to gain their trust so she could study with a

Maroon medicine man. Her patience was finally rewarded when the medicine man began to reveal his amazing powers. He told her about certain potions and poisons found in the wild that had beneficial medicinal and healing qualities. As always, Hurston wanted to learn by participating, and she was allowed to participate in spiritual ceremonies. Although Hurston found Jamaica to be a color-conscious and sexist culture, she was able to collect some valuable Jamaican folklore.

Hurston's next visit was to Haiti, where she accomplished two very important goals: One was to explore the mysterious, dark world of voodoo. The second was to begin work on her second book of fiction, *Their Eyes Were Watching God.*

Hurston's experiences with the voodoo religion had a profound effect on her, both physically and spiritually. Although Roman Catholicism is the official religion of Haiti, many followers of voodoo consider it to be a form of religion with its own unique beliefs and ceremonies. The word "voodoo" is an African name for a god or sacred object. It involves the spirits of long-gone ancestors, and its ceremonies are presided over by a high priest or priestess.

Hurston was so impressed with voodoo ceremonies that she wrote in her autobiography, "I did not find [the voodoo ceremonies in Haiti] any more invalid than any other religion. Rather, I hold that any religion that satisfies the individual urge is valid for that person."[1]

Eager to get to work, Hurston rented a house in Port-au-Prince in September 1936. She hoped that this trip would be just as successful as the Jamaican one, and she was not disappointed. In fact, there was such an abundance of material that Hurston was overwhelmed by the formidable task. She learned that voodoo was an important part of Haitian culture. She was even warned not to take voodoo lightly because of the good and bad gods, whose powers were all-encompassing. She also was told to be careful of the "Petro gods," who were similar to the devil.[2]

Hurston listened to the warnings, but she was an adventurous soul, and continued with her research until June 1937, when she became ill with a stomach ailment. She was confined to bed for two weeks. Although Hurston was not a superstitious person, she did believe in the powers of voodoo. Was it possible that voodoo was causing her illness, or were her old intestinal problems just flaring up again? In any case, she decided to stop her intense research, and concentrated on putting her notes into order. She had been fortunate in discovering an abundance of rich material on this fascinating religion. She had even photographed Felicia Felix-Mentor, who had died in 1907 and allegedly came back to life as a zombie in 1936.

In addition to collecting the voodoo material, Hurston had also managed to write her second novel, in just seven weeks. She poured her heart and soul into this book, releasing a flood of emotions into the love story of Janie Crawford and Tea Cake Woods. She quickly sent the manuscript to Lippincott, which accepted it for publication.

Hurston admitted that although the plot of *Their Eyes Were Watching God* was not her own life story, she did try to portray Janie and Tea Cake's love for each other with all the tenderness and love she felt for A. W. P. Janie Crawford's story is not just one of finding love and happiness. It is also a story of keeping one's own identity within a close relationship.

After several more months in Haiti, Hurston returned to the United States in the spring of 1937. She reached New York in September, just in time for the reviews of her book. As her first novel, *Jonah's Gourd Vine*, did, her second book also received mixed reviews.

Richard Wright, the author of *Native Son*, said, "[Hurston] exploits the phase of Negro life which is 'quaint.'"[3]

A much kinder review was written by Lucille Tompkins of *The New York Times*. She said:

This is Hurston's third novel, again about her own people—and it is beautiful. It is about Negroes, and a good deal of it is written in dialect, but it is really about everyone, or least [*sic*] everyone who isn't so civilized that he has not lost the capacity for glory.[4]

Although Hurston's talent was never in question, the presentation of her material was inevitably attacked as "primitive," or lacking in "social consciousness." Many of Hurston's peers felt she was ignoring the real problems of African Americans. Her critics wanted to see stories of social injustice, inequality, and prejudice against African Americans. They neglected to see the value in Hurston's depiction of a strong, articulate, African-American woman striving to discover her inner self.

Hurston, after all, was drawing upon her own experiences. She hoped that her work would be interpreted on a larger scale. Hurston did not agree with her fellow writers that she was making light of the unique problems facing African Americans. She saw her work as a celebration of African Americans. All she could do was to continue with her work, writing about those things that affected her the most.

In 1938, Hurston's fourth book was published by Lippincott. *Tell My Horse* is a collection of travel advice for travelers in Haiti, voodoo customs and folklore, and information on zombies. Unfortunately, *Tell My Horse* was received poorly in the literary community, and it sold poorly.

During this time, Hurston had also joined the Florida Federal Writers' Project, a government program started in 1935 as part of the Works Progress Administration to give jobs to unemployed authors during the Depression. She was put to work on a book project, *The Florida Negro*. Hurston contributed some of her own collected folktales and songs to this book, as well as stories collected by other staff members. Hurston stayed with the FWP for almost a year and a half, finishing in the summer of 1939.

Although Hurston was busy with her research and writing, she still found the time to marry again. On June 27, 1939, she married Albert Price, III, a man twenty-five years her junior. Hurston spent little time with Price. They did not get along well, and they were divorced four years later.

In November 1939, Hurston's fifth book, *Moses, Man of the Mountain*, was published. Hurston's Moses was endowed with mystical voodoo powers. He was the son of an Egyptian princess. It was an ambitious undertaking for Hurston, and once again, this book was subject to mixed reviews. Most reviewers thought that *Moses* was a powerful piece of work, but perhaps too big an undertaking, even for the talented Hurston.

Within five years, Hurston had published five books, had produced several dance and song revues, and had written many short stories and articles. Despite all this, her money situation had not changed much. Although she had attained literary prominence as an African-American woman writer, none of her novels sold more than five thousand copies before going out of print, and her largest royalty check was less than $1,000. She often had to supplement her writing by taking other jobs, which included teaching, giving lectures, and even working as a story consultant for Paramount Studios.

By the early 1940s, Hurston was about fifty years old and still writing, but her career was starting to wind down. Lippincott suggested she write her autobiography, which Hurston was reluctant to do, saying that her career was hardly over. Finally she agreed to write it. In the spring of 1941, she moved to California where she stayed with Katharine Mershon, a friend. By midsummer, she had written a first draft, and she then took a year to rewrite it. Writing about her life did not come easily to Hurston. She was not altogether truthful about certain facts. She wrote that she was nine when her mother died, but she was closer to thirteen, and her age was always said to be at least ten years less than it really was. Her friend Fannie Hurst referred to Hurston as a "woman half in shadow."[5]

Dust Tracks on a Road was published in November 1942, and won the *Saturday Review*'s Anisfield-Wolf Award for promoting race relations. Hurston received a prize of $1,000, and her picture appeared on the cover of *Saturday Review* magazine. Even with this award, her autobiography was criticized, mainly by black critics, for its neglect of the race problem, and for being less than honest. She was accused of writing for a white audience and recording only what they wanted to hear.

Hurston retorted by saying that she saw life through the eyes of a person, and did not wish to be a sociologist.[6] Growing weary of all the disparaging remarks, Hurston decided to move to Daytona Beach, Florida, for a quieter lifestyle. She bought a thirty-two-foot-long houseboat called *Wanago*, and she began to travel the Florida waterways. Although she was away from the literary influences of New York City, Hurston had no intention of giving up writing. Instead, she was just taking some time off to regain her physical and emotional strength. She soaked up the Florida sunshine and fished in the clear, blue waters, leaving the worries of the big city behind.

Chapter 9

SOLITUDE

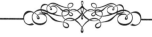

For the next four years Hurston traveled the Halifax and Indian Rivers on the *Wanago*. She rented a boat berth in Daytona Beach, and spent her days writing and fishing. The warm Florida sunshine helped Hurston's fragile state of health. In addition to her repeated bouts of intestinal problems, she had also contracted malaria on a previous trip near the Gulf of Mexico.

During the 1940s, Hurston wrote more than twenty articles for such magazines as the *Negro Digest*, *Saturday Review*, *Saturday Evening Post*, *Journal of American Folk*lore, and others. For those people who criticized Hurston for not recognizing or addressing the race problem, her published articles were proof of her deep thought and concern for African Americans.

Some of the articles she wrote were "What White Publishers Won't Print," "I Saw Negro Votes Peddled," "The Transplanted Negro," and "My Most Humiliating Jim Crow Experience."

During her lifetime, Hurston wrote more than fifty magazine articles, most of them concerning race relations. As early as 1928, Hurston had published an article in *World Tomorrow* entitled, "How It Feels to Be Colored Me." She wrote:

> I have no separate feeling about being an American Citizen and colored. I am merely a fragment of the Great Soul that surges within the boundaries. . . . Sometimes, I feel discriminated against, but it does not make me angry. It merely astonishes me. How *can* any deny themselves the pleasure of my company?[1]

Hurston's unique experience in growing up in an all-black town had a significant influence on her self-esteem and on the way she viewed her own and other races. Unlike other African Americans of her time, who were experiencing injustice, prejudice, and segregation, Hurston was not exposed to the effects of race discrimination until she left the protective embrace of her hometown. In her autobiography, she wrote about her feelings on the issue of race:

> I have no race prejudice of any kind. My kinfolks, and my 'skin-folks' are dearly loved. . . . So I give you all my right hand of fellowship and love, and hope for the same from you. In my eyesight, you lose nothing by not looking just like me.[2]

Hurston enjoyed the solitude and freedom of life that river living offered. In addition to regaining her strength, she was also working on a new novel called *Mrs. Doctor*. Yet even this contented lifestyle could not keep her in one place for too long. There were other commitments, other places to visit, and, always, the task of earning money.

In 1943, Zora Neale Hurston traveled to Washington, D.C., to receive Howard University's Annual Distinguished Alumni Award, and in 1944, she went to New York to collaborate on a musical comedy based on material from *Mules and Men* and other works. As soon as this business was taken care of, she went back to Florida, and later, she took *Wanago* on a fifteen-hundred-mile trip back to New York, hoping to find financial backing for the musical.

Hurston's sense of adventure took her to many places. In the mid-1940s, she was determined to visit the jungles of Honduras so she could search for the mysterious lost ruins of a famed Mayan city. Of course, first she had to raise money for the trip, and she applied for help from the Guggenheim Foundation. In the meantime, she continued to relax aboard her boat while fishing in the warm Florida waters.

Meanwhile, her old problem of recurring stomach ailments started to flare up again. In addition to this problem, she also developed stomach ulcers, which caused her considerable pain and discomfort. In spite of these problems, she was still eager to travel to Honduras. It was only her lack of funds, rather than the medical problems, that prevented her from doing so. Her book, *Mrs. Doctor*, had been rejected by Lippincott, and once again Hurston had to leave for New York, hoping to find a paying job.

Finally, Hurston's friend, author Marjorie Kinnan Rawlings, provided her an opportunity to change publishers. Rawlings' publisher, Charles Scribner's Sons, agreed to purchase Hurston's next book and offered her advance money. Hurston wasted no time in making plans to leave for Honduras. In the spring of 1947, she arrived in Puerto Cortes, where she rented a room in the Hotel Cosenza, and managed to do some exploring without spending all of her advance.

For the most part, Hurston stayed at the hotel and worked on her novel, *Seraph on the Suwanee*, a book about a white southern married couple and their ups and downs throughout their marriage. It was her first attempt to write about the whites. By September 1947, she sent a first draft to Scribner's and hoped to resume her exploration of Honduras.

In late February 1948, Hurston traveled back to New York, and on October 11, her last novel was published. Predictably, Hurston's new book again received mixed reviews. She had been proud of her other books, but had doubts about this one, which she expressed to her friend Marjorie Kinnan Rawlings. She was not so sure she had done her best with this one.[3] Had she been as successful in portraying the white race as she had been in portraying her own?

Worth Tuttle Hedden of the *New York Herald Tribune* Weekly wrote, "Miss Hurston knows her Florida Negro as she knows her Florida white and she characterizes them with the same acumen but she gives them no more attention than the plot demands."[4]

In any event, the book sold well, but in this same year, something else happened that cast a cloud over the pleasant experience of having her fourth novel published.

In September 1948, Hurston was charged with indecent behavior with a ten-year-old boy. The child's mother, who had once been Hurston's landlady, made the accusations. Hurston had done nothing wrong to this family, other than advising the child's mother nearly two years earlier that perhaps she should take her son for psychiatric testing. Hurston had expressed her opinion of possible mental instability in the child and thought she was being helpful when she spoke to the mother.[5] However, the child's mother had been offended at the suggestion and wanted to get back at Hurston's intrusion into her child's life.

Scribner's obtained a lawyer for Hurston while she went into hiding in a Bronx city apartment. Although she pleaded innocent to the charges, citing that she had not been in the country for most of the time that the boy had claimed she abused him, Hurston was nevertheless indicted. Unfortunately, the situation was aggravated when an African-American employee of the courts gave the story to the New York African-American newspapers. For one, the *Baltimore Afro-American* newspaper's headlines jumped out at the reader in bold type: Novelist Arrested on Morals Charge.

In March of 1949, the charges were dropped, although Hurston felt that her reputation had already been soiled. In a letter she wrote to her friend Carl Van Vechten, she said, "I have always believed in the (essential and) eventual rightness of my country. . . . I have never lived an easy life, but struggled on and on to achieve my ideals."[6]

It took Hurston a while to overcome this traumatic experience, but her writing helped her to get through this difficult time. Fortunately, the false charges did not hurt book sales. Scribner's even paid her an advance on her next book. In addition to working on this book, Hurston was also giving serious thought to re-organizing another trip to Honduras to search for the lost Mayan city. She decided to head back to the warm, comforting Florida sunshine, where she and a friend, Fred Irvine, would try to save some money for the Honduras trip.

When Irvine could not raise his share of the money to finance the Honduras trip, and Hurston was just about out of her own money, she decided to stay in Miami, Florida. Soon she was forced to find a job in order to keep a roof over her head and food on the table. Hurston always acknowledged the fact that she did not know how to manage money. When she had it, she spent it, and when she did not, she worked hard to earn it.

By the time Hurston was fifty-eight years old, she had published extensively and had degrees from Howard University and Barnard College. In addition, she was known for her anthropological work in the field of African-American folklore.

Even so, she had to take a job as a maid for a wealthy family in order to survive. Due to her fierce pride and independence, Hurston often had to survive alone because she did not like to ask for help from friends or family. When the *Miami Herald* found that Hurston was working as a maid on Rivo Island, the newspaper's headlines blared out: Noted Author Working As a Maid. Hurston tried to joke about the situation explaining that a little hard work never hurt anyone, and that she needed a change from all that writing she had done.[7]

In reality, Hurston's quality of writing was not what it had been. The book she had been working on for Scribner's was not going well, but she continued until it was finished. The book was called *The Lives of Barney Turk*. Scribner's rejected the book, as well as her next one, *The Golden Bench of God*.

Fortunately, she sold an article to the *Saturday Evening Post* for $1,000. "A Negro Voter Sizes Up Taft," was one of many political essays she wrote during the early 1950s. The money gave Hurston a much needed reprieve. In 1951, she moved again to Eau Gallie, Florida, and rented the same one-room cabin in which Hurston had written *Mules and Men*.

At times, Hurston's political and social views were contrary to important issues of the time. One such issue was the 1954 Supreme Court desegregation decision *Brown v. the Board of Education of Topeka, Kansas*, which Hurston opposed. She believed in self-determination, in the premise that blacks could support and help themselves without the intervention of white people. No doubt, her own experience of living in an all-black, self-governing town led her to believe that African-Americans could teach each other, govern their own towns, and nurture each other's children. She viewed desegregation as a way of forcing whites and blacks to do things they did not want to do. However, many other African Americans did not have the benefits of growing up in Eatonville and did not feel the effects of a strong, productive African-American community. Although they favored desegregation, Hurston was adamant in her support of African-American institutions and black pride.

For the next five years, Hurston lived a contented life. She fixed up the cabin, worked in her garden planting pink verbena and poppies, and fished for crab and shrimp in the Indian River. She had a dog named Spot and fed the many birds who came to her feeder. In her sixties, Hurston was relaxing and enjoying the activities she had given up due to her writing and constant traveling.

Of course, she continued to write, producing some articles, and she even started a sequel to her autobiography, *Dust Tracks on a Road*.

By the middle of the 1950s, Hurston's health had deteriorated badly. She weighed more than two hundred pounds, and she suffered from high blood pressure. The rented cabin she had so lovingly made into a home was sold by the owner, and once again, she was without a place to call her own. It was ironic that during the month of May, when she was left homeless, she was also the recipient of an award for Education and Human Relations, from Bethune-Cookman College.

Always resilient, Hurston moved in 1956 to Cocoa Beach, Florida, where she found work as a librarian at Patrick Air Force Base. Her salary was less than $2 an hour. She was also working on a new novel, *Herod the Great*, a story about the struggle of the Jewish people for the liberation of humankind. Hurston hoped that it would be accepted for publication, but like her two previous books, this one was also rejected by Scribner's. Instead of feeling despondent over the book's rejection, Hurston accepted its fate. Perhaps ill health overshadowed any disappointment she may have felt.

After nearly a year at the air force base, Hurston was deemed overqualified for her position and was fired. Luckily, she was able to collect weekly unemployment checks of $26.

Hurston's final years were lived in Fort Pierce, Florida, where she found work writing pieces for the *Fort Pierce Chronicle* and doing substitute teaching at Lincoln Park Academy. She lived in a rent-free, green concrete fifty-foot-square house owned by her doctor, C. C. Benton, who visited Hurston often, bringing her food and offering companionship. Her health grew steadily worse, but Hurston continued to work on the *Herod* book, still hoping to find a publisher for it.

In early 1959, Hurston suffered a stroke. She was able to continue on her own for a while, until May 1959, when she had to apply for welfare to pay for food and medicine. Always a proud person, she refused to ask friends and relatives for help. Earlier, she had even refused to attend a family reunion because she did not want anyone to know how ill she was.

On October 29, 1959, Hurston had to be admitted to the Saint Lucie County Welfare Home. On January 28, 1960, at the age of sixty-nine, Zora Neale Hurston died of heart disease. Friends raised the needed money for funeral costs. Hurston was buried in an unmarked grave in the Garden of the Heavenly Rest, a segregated cemetery in Fort Pierce.

Hurston's views on life and death were always philosophical and filled with insight. In her autobiography, she wrote, "I know that nothing is destructible: things merely change forms. . . Why fear? The stuff of my being is matter, ever changing, ever moving, but never lost."[8]

Chapter 10

REMEMBERED

Although Hurston traveled extensively and never stayed in one place for very long, she nevertheless kept in touch with her large family. As one of her nieces said, "She would just pop up, and we accepted her for who she was."[1]

At the age of fourteen, Hurston had embarked on a nontraditional, independent lifestyle. Placed in the position of having to take care of herself when her mother died, Hurston grew accustomed to doing whatever she pleased without having to answer to anyone but herself. She continued this way of life throughout adulthood, moving to a new town or state, or traveling out of the country, on a moment's notice. Hurston's sense of independence did not devalue the importance of family and friends, however. She tried to keep in touch with her many nieces and nephews by writing letters and sending cards.

Perhaps Hurston had never forgotten the agony of losing her mother and home and being sent to live with different friends and relatives. It is not widely known that Hurston took her sister's eight-year-old daughter, Zora Mack, into her New York City home when Sarah died of pneumonia in the late 1920s. Many years later, Zora Mack recalled how her aunt had bought her clothes and treated her with kindness. When her father remarried, Zora Mack went back home, but she always remembered the generosity of her Aunt Zora.[2]

In the 1930s, Hurston once again came to her nieces' rescue when her brother Bob died and his wife needed help with their daughters. First Wilhemina, and then Winifred, went to live with Hurston in Eatonville. The two girls recalled how pleasant and interesting their aunt had been, and how they enjoyed staying with her.[3]

Hurston's position within the family remained strong. She was admired and well liked by her nieces and nephews, who remember her as an important person who liked to tell stories.[4] Her family also respected her need for privacy and independence.

Hurston's family members were not the only ones who remembered her with affection and respect. In the early 1970s, the noted novelist Alice Walker became aware of Zora Neale Hurston's work through a few dedicated teachers who were using Hurston's work in their classrooms. Walker wanted to know more about this underrated writer, and why she was not well known within the literary and academic community. After reading Hurston's work, especially *Their Eyes Were Watching God*, Walker said, "[This book] speaks to me as no novel, past or present, has ever done."[5]

When Walker found out that Hurston had been buried in an unmarked grave, she decided to travel to the South to find the grave site. She was stunned that such a brilliant writer's grave did not have a headstone.

Walker wrote about her experience in a 1975 article, "Looking for Zora," which was published in *Ms.* magazine. She described her 1973 visit to the Garden of the Heavenly Rest Cemetery; it was "filled with bushes and weeds as tall as her waist, and she worried about snakes hiding in the tall grass."[6] Since there was no marker, Walker looked to where the ground was sunken to find the approximate grave site. Satisfied that she had come close to locating Hurston's grave, she then drove to a monument company and ordered a simple granite headstone. The simple inscription reads: Zora

Neale Hurston, A Genius of the South, Novelist, Folklorist, Anthropologist, 1901–1960. This inscription was taken from a poem by African-American writer Jean Toomer. The birth date may be incorrect. No one really knows when Hurston was born, since the birth documents were destroyed, and Hurston herself was secretive about her age. One family member says that Hurston was probably born in 1891.[7]

Until the 1970s, not much was known about Hurston's life, other than the information in the autobiography she had published in 1942. Most of her books had gone out of print. Then, in 1977, editor and writer Robert Hemenway published a comprehensive biography of Zora Neale Hurston. He spent eight years researching, writing, and traveling around the country in order to reaffirm the important contribution that Hurston's work had made to African-American culture, as well as to American literature.

Thanks to Alice Walker, Robert Hemenway, and other writers, Hurston's work has experienced a revival. Today, in colleges around the country, she is among the most widely taught African-American women writers. Her once-criticized usage of African-American dialect has not hindered a renewed interest in the naturalness of her prose.

Recently, the Library of America has published a collection of Hurston's work, making her the first African-American woman to receive such attention.

The literary community and the academic world have not been alone in recognizing Hurston's contribution to American literature and southern black folklore. In 1981, a Zora Neale Hurston Society was founded by Ruth Sheffey, a professor of English at Morgan State University in Baltimore, Maryland. The society numbers more than three hundred members.

Eatonville, Florida, has also honored its most famous resident. In January 1990, the first annual Zora Festival of the Arts was organized to honor Hurston. Many people who in one way or another had been touched by Hurston attended the festival. Alice Walker was present, along with Robert Hemenway and Ruby Dee, an actress who was to star in a play based on Hurston's life. Also in attendance were many of Hurston's relatives. Even Louise Thompson, who had worked with Langston Hughes and Hurston on *Mule Bone*, was there.

The festival was a happy celebration. Visitors were greeted with large colorful banners spelling out ZORA. There were games for the children, African-American crafts on display, and plenty of food for everyone. In addition, a memorial in Hurston's honor was dedicated by the Association to Preserve the Eatonville Community.

The festival also gave Hurston's family members a chance to reunite; some meeting each other there for the first time. It was an opportunity for them to say that they had cared about Zora Neale Hurston, and had offered to help her when she was sick and out of money.

Vivian Bowden, daughter of Zora's brother Clifford Joel, recalled how she and her parents drove to Fort Pierce, Florida, to see if her aunt needed anything. As was typical of Hurston, she said she was fine and did not need a thing.

Although Hurston chose to live a solitary life in her last years, she had not been deserted. When she would allow help, friends and family were glad to offer it. Marjorie Alden, a newspaper reporter, was one of those who befriended Hurston and invited her to dinners. Hurston's doctor, Clem C. Benton, let Hurston live rent-free in the small green concrete house in Fort Pierce.

After Hurston's death, Margaret Paige, a secretary at Lincoln Park Academy, raised money to pay for her burial, and Alden helped to arrange the funeral. The best place for Hurston to have been buried was in Eatonville, but without the consent of her remaining siblings, who could not be located, this was impossible, so she was buried in Fort Pierce.

What would Hurston have thought of her revival as an important African-American woman writer of the 1990s? Her intuition that she would always remain a part of the world had been fulfilled. With help from friends and family, Zora Neale Hurston is once again with us, and rightfully so. Many have come to honor the work and memory of the Eatonville girl whose mother had told her to "jump at the sun."

CHRONOLOGY

1891—Born in Eatonville, Florida.

1904—Lucy Ann Potts Hurston, Zora's mother, dies when Zora is thirteen years old.

1906—Hurston works as a lady's maid for "Miss M," an actress in a Gilbert and Sullivan acting troupe.

1917—Hurston attends Morgan Academy in Baltimore and receives her diploma.

1919—Hurston attends Howard University in Washington, D.C.

1920—Earns associate degree from Howard University.

1921—Hurston publishes her first story, "John Redding Goes to Sea," in the Howard University literary magazine, *The Stylus*.

1925—Hurston wins second place awards for short story, "Spunk," and a play, *Color Struck*, in a contest sponsored by *Opportunity* magazine; attends Barnard College in New York.

1926—The magazine *Fire!!*, published by Hurston, Langston Hughes, and other writers, debuted and ended with the November issue.

1927—Graduates from Barnard College; takes her first folklore-collecting trip to Florida; meets Charlotte Mason; later, signs a contract with Mason to finance her folklore-collecting trips and writing; marries Herbert Sheen.

1930—Collaborates with Langston Hughes on the play *Mule Bone*.

1931—Has disagreement with Hughes over *Mule Bone* and breaks off their working relationship; divorces Herbert Sheen.

1932—Produces a stage revue, *The Great Day*, performed on January 10 at the John Golden Theatre in New York.

1934—Mary McLeod Bethune asks her to come to Bethune-Cookman College to establish a school of dramatic arts based on black expression; publishes first book of fiction, *Jonah's Gourd Vine*.

1935—Second book, *Mules and Men*, is published.

1936—Goes to Jamaica to collect folklore; goes to Haiti to research voodoo; writes third book, *Their Eyes Were Watching God*.

1937—*Their Eyes Were Watching God* is published.

1938—Fourth book, *Tell My Horse*, is published; joins Federal Writers' Project.

1939—Marries Albert Price, III; fifth book, *Moses Man of the Mountain*, is published.

1942—Publishes her autobiography, *Dust Tracks on a Road*.

1943—Receives the Anisfield-Wolf Book Award in Race Relations for *Dust Tracks on a Road*; divorces Albert Price, III; moves to Florida; receives Howard University's Annual Distinguished Alumni Award.

1947—Goes to Puerto Cortes, Honduras, to explore and work on book.

1948—Final book, *Seraph on the Suwanee*, is published; falsely accused of a morals charge.

1949—False morals charges are dismissed.

1951—Moves to Eau Gallie, Florida, and lives happily there for five years.

1956—Takes a job as a librarian at Patrick Air Force Base in Cocoa Beach, Florida.

1958—Becomes a substitute teacher at Lincoln Park Academy in Fort Pierce, Florida.

1959—Health declines; suffers a stroke; enters Saint Lucie County Welfare Home.

1960—Dies on January 28, at the Welfare Home; is buried in an unmarked grave in the Garden of Heavenly Rest in Fort Pierce.

1973—Writer Alice Walker finds Hurston's grave and buys a granite headstone to mark it.

1991—Eatonville, Florida, holds its first Zora Neale Hurston Festival.

CHAPTER NOTES

Chapter 1. New York, Here I Come

1. Mary E. Lyons, *Sorrow's Kitchen: The Life and Folklore of Zora Neale Hurston* (New York: Collier Books, 1993), p. 35.

2. Paul Witcover, *Zora Neale Hurston: Author* (Los Angeles: Melrose Square Publishing Co., 1994), p. 31.

3. Zora Neale Hurston, *Dust Tracks on a Road* (New York: HarperCollins Publishing, 1991) (originally published 1942), p. 255.

Chapter 2. Home—Eatonville, Florida

1. Paul Witcover, *Zora Neale Hurston: Author* (Los Angeles: Melrose Square Publishing Co., 1991), p. 31.

2. Ibid., p. 37.

3. Robert E. Hemenway, *Zora Neale Hurston: A Literary Biography* (Chicago: University of Illinois Press, 1977), p. 16.

4. Witcover, p. 50.

5. Mary E. Lyons, *Sorrow's Kitchen: The Life and Folklore of Zora Neale Hurston* (New York: Collier Books, 1993), p. 20.

Chapter 3. It's a Hard Life

1. Paul Witcover, *Zora Neale Hurston: Author* (Los Angeles: Melrose Square Publishing Co., 1991), p. 50.

2. Zora Neale Hurston, *Dust Tracks on a Road* (New York: HarperCollins Publishing, 1991) (originally published 1942), p. 109.

3. Ibid.

Chapter 4. A Literary and Academic World

1. Robert E. Hemenway, *Zora Neale Hurston: A Literary Biography* (Chicago: University of Illinois Press, 1977), p. 36.

2. Zora Neale Hurston, *Dust Tracks on a Road* (New York: HarperCollins Publishing, 1991) (originally published 1942), p. 225.

3. Ibid., p. 176.

4. Ibid., p. 124.

Chapter 5. In New Directions

1. Robert E. Hemenway, *Zora Neale Hurston: A Literary Biography* (Chicago: University of Illinois Press, 1977), pp. 93–94.

2. Paul Witcover, *Zora Neale Hurston: Author* (Los Angeles: Melrose Square Publishing Co., 1991), p. 109.

3. Hemenway, p. 107.

4. Ibid., p. 108.

5. Ibid., p. 111.

6. Zora Neale Hurston, *Dust Tracks on a Road* (New York: HarperCollins Publishing, 1991) (originally published 1942), p. 139.

7. Ibid.

Chapter 6. The *Mule Bone* Controversy

1. Robert E. Hemenway, *Zora Neale Hurston: A Literary Biography* (Chicago: University of Illinois Press, 1977), pp. 139.

2. Ibid., p. 141.

3. Ibid., p. 142.

4. Langston Hughes and Zora Neale Hurston, *Mule Bone: A Comedy of Negro Life* (New York: HarperCollins Publishing, 1991), p. 10.

Chapter 7. The Writing Life

1. Zora Neale Hurston, *Dust Tracks on a Road* (New York: HarperCollins Publishing, 1991) (originally published 1942), p. 153.

2. Ibid., p. 154.

3. Henry Louis Gates, Jr., and K. A. Appiah, eds., *Zora Neale Hurston: Critical Perspectives Past and Present* (New York: Amistad Press, 1993), p. 4.

4. Ibid., p. 9.

5. Robert E. Hemenway, *Zora Neale Hurston: A Literary Biography* (Chicago: University of Illinois Press, 1977), p. 201.

6. Ibid., pp. 206–207.

7. Hurston, pp. 184–185.

Chapter 8. Different Worlds

1. Zora Neale Hurston, *Dust Tracks on a Road* (New York: HarperCollins Publishing, 1991) (originally published 1942), p. 149.

2. Robert E. Hemenway, *Zora Neale Hurston: A Literary Biography* (Chicago: University of Illinois Press, 1977), p. 247.

3. Henry Louis Gates, Jr., and K. A. Appiah, eds. *Zora Neale Hurston: Critical Perspectives Past and Present* (New York: Amistad Press, 1993), p. 17.

4. Ibid., p. 18.

5. Tiffany R. L. Patterson, "Zora Neale Hurston" in *Black Women in America: An Historical Encyclopedia,* vol. 1 (New York: Carlson Publishing, Inc., 1993), p. 602.

6. Paul Witcover, *Zora Neale Hurston: Author* (Los Angeles: Melrose Square Publishing Co., 1991), p. 171.

Chapter 9. Solitude

1. Alice Walker, ed. *I Love Myself When I Am Laughing. . . and Then Again When I Am Looking Mean and Impressive* (New York: Feminist Press, 1979), p. 155.

2. Zora Neale Hurston, *Dust Tracks on a Road* (New York: HarperCollins Publishing, 1991) (originally published 1942), p. 209.

3. Robert E. Hemenway, *Zora Neale Hurston: A Literary Biography* (Chicago: University of Illinois Press, 1977), p. 315.

4. Henry Louis Gates, Jr., and K. A. Appiah, eds., *Zora Neale Hurston: Critical Perspectives Past and Present* (New York: Amistad Press, 1993), pp. 34–35.

5. Paul Witcover, *Zora Neale Hurston: Author* (Los Angeles: Melrose Square Publishing Co., 1991), p. 176.

6. Hemenway, p. 322.

7. Ibid., p. 325.

8. Hurston, pp. 202–203.

Chapter 10. Remembered

1. N.Y. Nathiri, *Zora! Zora Neale Hurston: A Woman and Her Community* (Orlando, Fla.: Sentinel Communications Co., 1991), p. 65.

2. Ibid., p. 63.

3. Ibid., p. 64.

4. Ibid., pp. 66–67.

5. Alice Walker, ed., *I Love Myself When I Am Laughing . . . and Then Again When I Am Looking Mean and Impressive* (New York: Feminist Press, 1979), p. 2.

6. Ibid., p. 305.

7. Robert E. Hemenway, *Zora Neale Hurston: A Literary Biography* (Chicago: University of Illinois Press, 1977), p. 13.

FURTHER READING

Books

Fradin, Dennis Brindell and Judith Bloom Fradin. *Zora!: The Life of Zora Neale Hurston.* New York: Clarion Books, 2012.

Lyons, Mary E. Sorrow's Kitchen: *The Life and Folklore of Zora Neale Hurston.* New York: Atheneum Books for Young Readers, 1993.

Marsico, Katie. *Zora Neale Hurston: Harlem Renaissance Writer.* Edina, Minn.: Abdo Publishing Company, 2008.

Sapet, Kerrily. *Rhythm and Folklore: The Story of Zora Neale Hurston.* Greensboro, N.C.: Morgan Reynolds Publishing, 2008.

Stefoff, Rebecca and Ronald Takaki. *A Different Mirror for Young People: A History of Multicultural America.* New York: Seven Stories Press, 2012.

Yates, Janelle. *Zora Neale Hurston: A Storyteller's Life.* Staten Island, N.Y.: Ward Hill Press, 1993.

Books by Zora Neale Hurston

Hurston, Zora Neale. *Dust Tracks on a Road.* New York: HarperCollins, 1991. Reprint of the edition published by J. B. Lippincott, 1942.

———. *Jonah's Gourd Vine.* Philadelphia: J. B. Lippincott, 1934. Reprinted, Philadelphia: J. B. Lippincott, 1971.

———. *Moses Man of the Mountain*. Philadelphia: J. B. Lippincott, 1939. Reprinted, Chatham, N.J.: Chatham Bookseller, 1974.

———. *Mules and Men*. Philadelphia: J. B. Lippincott, 1935. Reprinted, New York: Negro University Press, 1969. Reprinted, New York: Harper and Row, 1970.

———. *Seraph on the Suwanee*. New York: Charles Scribner's Sons, 1948. Reprinted, Ann Arbor, Mich.: University Microfilms, 1971. Reprinted, New York: AMS Press, 1974.

———. *Their Eyes Were Watching God*. Philadelphia: J. B. Lippincott, 1937. Reprinted, New York: Negro University Press, 1969. Reprinted, Urbana: University of Illinois Press, 1978.

———. *Tell My Horse: Voodoo and Life in Haiti and Jamaica*. Philadelphia: J. B. Lippincott, 1938. Reprinted, New York ETC, 1938. Reprinted, New York Perennial Library, 1990.

INDEX